The Valley of tl

H. C. McNeile

Alpha Editions

This edition published in 2024

ISBN : 9789362926302

Design and Setting By
Alpha Editions
www.alphaedis.com
Email - info@alphaedis.com

As per information held with us this book is in Public Domain. This book is a reproduction of an important historical work. Alpha Editions uses the best technology to reproduce historical work in the same manner it was first published to preserve its original nature. Any marks or number seen are left intentionally to preserve its true form.

THE VALLEY OF THE SHADOW

For the twentieth time Hilda Garling asked herself the same question—Why had her husband asked Jack Denver to stay? Mechanically she helped herself to some dish which the footman was handing to her, hardly knowing what it was she took. Why had he asked Jack to stay?

Such a thing was so completely foreign to her husband's habits of late. For the last year or so he had grown more and more of a recluse, shutting himself away for hours and even days at a time, and having his meals served in his own room, until the big house standing back from the Portsmouth road had seemed a veritable prison to his wife. Not that it was much better when her husband did come out of his seclusion, but at any rate he was a human being of her own class.

She had tried asking people to stay, but it wasn't a success. When your host plainly shows you that your presence fails to amuse him, even the most thick-skinned guest begins to look up the trains for London. She had tried going away to stay with friends, but that was only a temporary panacea. And then a year ago even that relief had been denied her. Her husband had complained once or twice of a pain in the chest, and although he scouted the idea that it was anything but indigestion, he at length agreed to do as she wished and send for a doctor. And the doctor had spoken to her after his examination.

"Mrs. Garling," he said, "I am sorry to have to be the bearer of—I won't say bad, but of serious news. It is no mere question of indigestion, I fear. It is heart trouble—and it is pronounced. Please understand me. There is no reason, if your husband lives a quiet life and avoids excitement or undue exertion of all sorts, why he shouldn't live for another twenty or thirty years. But any sudden physical call on his system—and the chances are, I am afraid, it would kill him."

"Have you told my husband?" she asked him.

"Not quite as clearly as I have told you," answered the doctor. "But he is fully aware that his condition is more serious than he thought."

From that time on she had hardly ever slept a night away from the Pines. For Hilda Garling had the instinct of playing the game very fully developed. It was hypocrisy to pretend to herself that she loved him: looking back on the five years of their married life she realized that she never had loved him. Like so many girls fresh from the schoolroom, she had been captivated by a brilliantly clever and handsome man some fourteen years older than herself. She had thought herself in love with him, and her parents, having inquired into Hubert Garling's social and financial status, and having found both—especially the latter—eminently satisfactory, had put no obstacle in the way of what seemed to them a very desirable match.

But even before the honeymoon was over disillusion had begun to set in. That Hubert had a jealous nature she had found out while they were engaged, and then she had been rather flattered by it. But until they were married she never realized how fiendishly jealous he was. Once at Nice, as they were on their way home, she had danced twice with a young French officer, and the scene that night in their room had been appalling. It had blown over, as such scenes do, but it had left an indelible mark. It had frightened the girl—she was still only a child at the time; but it had hastened her mental development far more than a year of ordinary life. To her amazement she had found herself listening to Hubert's whispered apologies and love-makings with only half her mind. The other half was disconcertingly cold and logical.

"This is insulting," it said. "You may be his; in a way, since you're his wife, you are. But an outlook on life that forbids you to dance with someone else, and gets furious if you do, is mediæval."

As time went on it got no better. The slightest sign of interest in another man was sufficient to precipitate either a furious scene or sullenness, until Hilda for very peace' sake confined her male acquaintanceship to the old vicar of seventy-two and the doctor, who was three years younger. And the absurd thing about it all was that there had never been the tiniest particle of justification for her husband's attitude; never, that is, until—

Again she asked herself the question—Why had he asked Jack Denver to stay? He was talking now to his guest in that charming, well-bred manner of his that had captivated so many people—talking well and interestingly, as a glance at Jack's face revealed, though she hadn't heard a word that had been said for the last ten minutes. It was incredible, impossible, that Hubert could know; after all, what was there to know? Six months ago, on one of her rare visits to London, she had stayed the night with an old school friend—Joan Prettyman. Mr. Prettyman, Joan's father, had tactfully gone up to Manchester on business, and Joan had greeted her with a shout of joy.

"My dear," she cried, "in you lies salvation! Cecil Turnbury, who dances like an angel, rang me up this morning to dine and wine, do a show, trek on to Ciro's, and come home with the milk from a night club. I know it will come to the old man's ears if I go alone with Cecil; you must come, too. I'll ring up Cecil now, and tell him to rope in a cheery soul for you."

For a moment or two she had feebly protested; she couldn't dance—her husband—she must get back.

"Tripe!" remarked Joan, elegantly, and forthwith rang up Cecil. And he had arrived at seven-thirty with Jack Denver. From the outset of the evening it was quite clear what was going to happen. Joan, having taken the possible wind out of father's sails, devoted herself exclusively to Cecil, leaving Jack Denver and Hilda to carry on their share of the good work. And Hilda, starved, though she hardly realized it, for the companionship of men of her own age, had the night of her life. There are nights which stand out like milestones in every life, and almost always are they impromptu. And there had been singularly few for Hilda Garling. But in those eight hours she realized fully for the first time all that she had missed in marrying Hubert.

Jack Denver was thirty and in the Army. Moreover, he was a man's man all through. London saw him but rarely, except when he was playing polo at Ranelagh or Hurlingham; he found that London life interfered with his eye. But in addition to being mad on every form of sport he was—without being clever—exceedingly intelligent. He was interested in politics and life generally; he read with discrimination. He could talk amusingly, and, most precious of all gifts, listen sympathetically. And that night, having gone merely to please Cecil and swearing he must be in bed by one, he found himself wishing at half-past three that it could go on for another four hours. From the time they arrived at Ciro's, it had been merely two duets.

From Ciro's they had driven to the night club in two taxis—Joan, being quite without shame, had insisted on that. And during the drive Jack Denver tried to take stock of matters. That Hilda was married he knew; that her husband was a bit of a rum 'un he knew also from Joan. But there was another thing also which he knew, and that was that never in the course of his life had he been so powerfully attracted by any woman before.

Small wonder. Hilda—enjoying herself to the hilt—looked utterly lovely. But it wasn't only a question of looks; she was so startlingly alive. The stagnation of months had boiled over in an immense reaction. And if there was one thing which Jack Denver worshipped, it was vitality.

They left the night club at half-past three, and once more two taxis were requisitioned.

"Have you enjoyed yourself?" he asked quietly as they drove off.

"It's been heaven!" she answered.

Which, taken as a conversational effort, would not have won a prize. But when the atmosphere is electrical, it doesn't much matter what is said.

"Mrs. Garling," he went on, gravely, "when may I see you again?"

By the light of a passing lamp she saw his eyes fixed on her, and her own did not falter.

"I don't think we'd better meet again," she said, steadily. "My husband has rather peculiar ideas on the subject."

"That, of course, is quite unthinkable," he remarked. "I have never enjoyed such a wonderful evening before."

"No more have I," she said, staring out of the window.

She felt his hand close over hers, and for a while she made no effort to remove it. Then with a little shiver she almost snatched her hand away.

"Captain Denver," she said, "this is folly. I must tell you that my husband is almost crazily jealous of me. If he were to know that you and I were driving home at this hour of the night in a taxi alone, I think he'd probably try to—try to kill me. It sounds incredible, but it's the truth. He becomes like a madman if I even speak to another man; in fact, there have been times when I really believe he has been out of his senses."

"But it's preposterous," he said, angrily. "He can't keep you shut up like a prisoner."

"He would if he could," she answered.

"A truce to this fooling, Hilda," said Denver, urgently. "We're nearly at your house. I must see you again; I *must*. It may be folly, or it may not. I know I only met you eight hours ago—what's that matter? Time has no meaning on some occasions. I'm being crude, too; I know that, but the circumstances make it imperative. May I motor over from Aldershot and call on you?"

The taxi was already slowing up.

"It's madness," she whispered, "absolute madness."

"Then I'm going to be mad," he remarked quietly, as the car stopped.

The other taxi was just behind them, and for a moment or two they all stood talking on the pavement. Then, with a prodigious yawn, Joan voted for bed, and the two girls went indoors.

"A gladsome night," she said, sleepily. "And it strikes me, Hilda, my dear, that for a little sheltered country rose you're a pretty high-class performer. He's a pet, that man Denver; in fact, I'd have changed over half-way through if I hadn't known there wasn't a look-in for little Joan. Did he kiss you in the bus coming home?"

"Joan—how can you ask such a thing?" cried Hilda, blushing furiously.

"Cut it out, my angel—cut it out. If he didn't he's a mutt—and so are you. Heigh-ho! bed for this child."

True to his word, Jack Denver drove his car over from Aldershot to the Pines three days later. He stayed to tea and talked more to Hubert than to her. And after tea he suggested a spin to Hindhead and the Devil's Punchbowl.

"I'm afraid an open car is one of the things I'm forbidden," said Hubert.

"Then what about you, Mrs. Garling?" asked Jack.

"My wife doesn't care about motoring," said her husband harshly.

A truly impossible fellow, reflected Jack, as he drove back to barracks. Charming in other respects—but on the subject of his wife quite impossible. And deep down inside a warning voice began to make itself heard—a voice that counselled caution. With a husband like that the most ordinary everyday politeness would be misconstrued. And Jack Denver was quite sufficiently honest with himself to realize that, if he saw much of Hilda Garling, he would have considerable difficulty in keeping things on the plane of conventional courtesy. In fact, as he dressed for mess that night he apostrophized his reflection in the glass in no uncertain manner.

"You're nine-tenths of the way towards falling in love with another man's wife. And that's a complication at the best of times. But, with a husband like that, it's the devil. So take a pull at yourself, young feller; take a pull."

And a pull he did take—for quite a fortnight. Then, as luck would have it, duty took him to Portsmouth. He couldn't get back to Aldershot the same night, and the following morning he started back in his car. And as he got near the Pines his pace grew slower and slower. Finally he stopped and lit a cigarette.

"Don't be a fool," said one voice. "Go on; there's polo at the club this afternoon."

"You've played polo every day for the last week," said another voice. "The man can't eat you if you ask for lunch. Don't be a coward."

And since it's better to be called a fool than a coward, the second voice won. Jack Denver went to the Pines for the second time. And when he left at about five o'clock the nine-tenths had changed to nineteen-twentieths.

Of course, the thing was a foregone conclusion. He got into the habit of going about once a week, and one day it all came out with a rush—like a stream that had been temporarily dammed.

They were in the garden—the two of them, and something seemed suddenly to snap.

"Come away with me, my darling," he muttered. "This man is an impossible husband for you. I've got plenty of money, and I'm chucking the service, anyhow."

He tried to take her in his arms, but she drew back.

"Don't, dear, don't," she said, a little breathlessly. "It's impossible."

"Why is it impossible?" he demanded. "You love me, Hilda—I know that. And I worship the very ground you walk on. Why is it impossible?"

"Because it would kill Hubert," she answered, steadily. "I've never told you before, Jack, but I must now. You merely thought he was delicate. It's his heart; and any sudden shock would kill him. And we couldn't do that, Jack—could we?"

"And if it wasn't for that?" he asked, dully.

She took a deep breath.

"If it wasn't for that, my man," she whispered, "I'd go to the end of the world with you to-morrow."

And, being a white man, Jack Denver merely raised her fingers to his lips and left her. It was final; it was unalterable, and it was not for him to make it harder. She heard his car drive away, and she gave a little sobbing cry. Then very steadily she walked into the house.

From that day to this she hadn't seen Jack; that had been all. All, that is, except one thing—the one thing which would have supplied the answer to her oft-repeated question. A minute after she had walked into the house a man stepped out of some bushes close to where she had been standing. At first glance it would have been hard to recognize who it was; his face was so distorted with devilish fury that he looked like a fiend. For a while he stood there, his fists tight clenched. Then he suddenly swayed, and instinctively one hand went to his heart. The fury was replaced by agony—which in its turn gave way to relief.

And shortly after Hubert Garling, outwardly calm, followed his wife indoors.

That had been three months ago. And three days ago he had done the amazingly unexpected thing.

They were having lunch, and he suddenly asked her about Jack.

"What's become of that nice fellow Denver?" he remarked. "We never seem to see him now."

"I don't know," she answered, calmly, though she felt that all the colour had left her face. "Perhaps he's on leave or manœuvres or something."

"Why don't you write and ask him to come over?" continued her husband. "Ask him over for the weekend."

"I'll write, certainly," she said, and wondered whether he could hear the pounding of her heart.

"The workmen are away from the tower, you know," he went on; "and he seemed an amusing chap."

"I'll write after lunch," she said, quietly.

And thus it came about that Jack Denver received the following morning a letter in a writing that made his hand shake uncontrollably as he opened the envelope.

"Hubert, for some astounding reason, is anxious for you to come and stay. As for me—I think I shall go mad I don't see you again soon. If you think it unwise, plead duty as an excuse. But I think you'll have to come soon, or else the sudden cessation of your visits here will make H. suspicious. Come for the weekend.

"H. G."

He stared at his untasted breakfast; then he shrugged his shoulders. So be it. And his answer was duly delivered at the Pines.

"Dear Mrs. Garling,—

"How charming of you! I fear you must have thought I was dead, but we do work—sometimes! I'll come in time for lunch on Saturday if I may.

"Yours sincerely,

"Jack Denver."

And now dinner was over, and she was still as far as ever from getting the answer to her question. Why had Hubert done it? All through the afternoon he had been uniformly charming; he couldn't suspect anything; he couldn't. He was talking now about the tower—a strange architectural freak which stuck up from one corner of the house like a funnel on a locomotive.

"It's an old house," he was saying in his cultured, rather gentle voice. "And I can't quite make out who erected that tower originally. It was put up after the house itself was built, but for what purpose is a little obscure. It certainly can't have been entirely erected as a tomb."

"A tomb!" echoed Denver in surprise. "In what way a tomb?"

"Has my wife never told you the story?" said Garling. "It's one of the stock things about this place. I can just remember when my father made the discovery. The tower, of course, is hollow, and it had been used as a sort of box-room. There were some rough steps going spirally round it which finished abruptly in the brick roof. And one day it struck my father that it was somewhat peculiar to make steps right up to a ceiling, and he took some measurements. And he found that there was a space of about ten feet to be accounted for at the top of the tower. You can understand, of course, that it was very rare indeed that any one went there, or such an obvious thing would have been discovered before. So he got in some workmen and proceeded to remove the bricks from the roof. And the mystery was solved. The steps which apparently disappeared into the ceiling were now found to communicate with a room. And in that room the remnants of two skeletons were found. They had been there for at least a hundred years, but there was enough to prove that one had been a man and the other a woman."

"How very interesting!" said Denver. "Did your father ever find out what had happened?"

"Not for absolutely certain," answered his host. "But I have no doubt in my own mind that it was the truth. Apparently this house, at the time when the man and woman died, belonged to a man called Shaw. And Mrs. Shaw was a very lovely lady—a fact which other men beside Mr. Shaw appreciated. Moreover, it appeared that Mrs. Shaw was not insensible to the admiration of those other men—especially to that of a young Lord Greyton. Possibly she was flattered by the attentions of a member of the aristocracy, since her husband, though an eminently worthy man, was distinctly middle-class. At any rate, she and Lord Greyton disappeared, and were never heard of again. Mr. Shaw gave out that his wife had eloped with him, and forbade her name ever to be mentioned in his presence again. But I think there can be little doubt that somehow or other he trapped them both into the room at the top of the tower, and then proceeded to brick them in. The details, of course, will never be known. Presumably he must have drugged them first, leaving them to regain consciousness in the black darkness—because there were no windows of any sort in the tower. One thing is certain: they were not dead when they were put there. The marks are plainly visible where they had endeavoured to scratch away the brickwork with their fingers."

"What an extraordinarily gruesome story!" said Denver. "Why, Mrs. Garling—you've gone quite pale."

"I think it's a horrible story," she said, in a low voice.

"Horrible—and yet full of poetic justice," remarked her husband, sipping his port.

"And what do you use the tower for now?" asked Denver.

"My father, who was a keen astronomer, had it made into a small observatory. I've left it much as it was, except that I've removed the telescope and carried out a few small improvements. In fact, the workmen have only just finished. My father, for instance, had a sliding roof; I've had that removed. There is now merely a small dome with thick glass at the top, through which one can get a gay wonderful view of the heavens."

He glanced at Denver's glass.

"Some more port? No. Well—would you care to come and see the actual room itself? And I particularly want you, my dear, to see it by artificial light." He turned to his wife. "I think you'll agree that it's an immense improvement. In fact, I'm seriously thinking of using it in future as my study. It's small, of course—in fact, tiny. But it's so far removed from any noise or disturbance. And I find, Denver, that I can concentrate better in a confined space."

He was leading the way along an upstair corridor as he talked.

"I am a bit of a recluse, and I write a little. Dull, scientific stuff. And I really believe that in this room I have got my ideal working room."

He had reached the top of the stairs in the tower and opened the door.

"Quaint, isn't it? Those Chinese hangings round the walls give it a cosy effect. And then this door—sound-proof. I cannot hear any noise when I'm at work."

They were standing in the centre of the room, and Jack Denver looked round with frank curiosity. It certainly was quaint. Above their heads, through the glass dome, he could see the sky glittering with stars—a magnificent view, as his host had said. A thick pile carpet covered the floor, and the only pieces of furniture were a heavy desk that filled half the room and a big chair. The electric light was concealed just where the dome commenced, and threw its direct rays upwards, giving a pleasant diffused light all over the room. And the walls— hexagonal in shape—were completely covered with rich yellow

Oriental silk panels. A bizarre room—almost an uncanny room; yet with a strange element of fascination about it.

"There was one thing I omitted to mention at dinner in my little story," said Hubert Garling. "From what small study I have made of the matter, there can be no doubt that Mrs. Shaw and Lord Greyton died of suffocation. In fact, I once made a calculation that the supply of air would have lasted them about twelve hours. This room is half the original size."

"Poor brutes!" remarked Denver.

"Moreover," continued his host, "the fact that Mr. Shaw was unable to watch their death struggle must have robbed his revenge of much of its charm."

For a moment they saw his face—distorted, fiendish; then the door shut, and they were alone. Half stupefied they stared at one another; the whole thing was so sudden, so utterly unexpected. And it was the girl who recovered herself first and spoke.

"He knew, Jack," she whispered. "He's known all along. That's why he made me ask you here."

Denver swore softly under his breath; as yet he had not realized the danger.

"Damn him!" he said, angrily. "This is beyond a joke. We've done absolutely nothing of which we need be ashamed. Why, I've never even kissed you, Hilda." He went to the door and tugged at it; it refused to budge.

"Well, this settles it, my dear," he went on. "He may have a weak heart or he may not—but I don't stand for this form of humour. I shall tell your husband exactly what I think of him, and that you're going to come away with me. And he can take what steps he damn well chooses."

He lit a cigarette and began pacing up and down the little room with short, angry steps, while the girl, leaning against the desk, watched him with a strange look in her eyes.

"Jack, dear," she said at length, "I don't think you quite understand. This isn't a joke."

He stopped short in his tracks and stared at her.

"What do you mean?" he asked, in a low voice.

"This is dead earnest. He means to murder us."

The colour slowly left his face.

"Murder us?" he stammered, foolishly.

"That's why he told you that story at dinner tonight. That's why he's had men working on this tower, and didn't suggest that you should come over till they'd finished. That's why he's locked us in here."

"But, good God! Hilda, the man must be mad," he said, hoarsely.

"On the subject of me he is," she answered.

And still it seemed as if he could hardly realize.

"But someone must come," he cried, angrily. "He can't keep us shut in here for days."

She went across to him.

"Didn't you hear what he said as he went out? Suffocation. It took twelve hours for those two, and this is half the size. Six hours, Jack—six hours. And the servants are on the other side of the house."

And now at last he understood, and with the understanding he became himself again. He smiled thoughtfully, and pressed out his cigarette.

"Under those circumstances—no smoking. And under those circumstances also—no scruples either."

He caught the girl in his arms and kissed her again and again, while she clung to him half sobbing. Then, still with the same thoughtful smile, he pushed her gently into the chair.

"I must explore," he said, briefly.

First of all—the door. Coolly he examined it, while the girl watched him with eager eyes. He seemed so calm and assured—so completely confident in himself.

A minute or two later he turned and looked at her.

"Nothing doing there," he said cheerfully. "It fits as tight as a safe door, and there isn't even a keyhole on this side. It must have some patent form of lock."

He went round the walls quietly and systematically, tearing down the silk panels as he got to them. Nothing but smooth cement—not a crack, not a fissure.

He stood on the desk to examine the roof. It was of flawless glass, immensely thick. And then he had to get down abruptly. He put his hand to his forehead; it was wet with perspiration.

And now the full gravity of the situation had come home to him. Mad, Hubert Garling might be; there was no sign of madness about this trap. It was diabolically efficient. It was small consolation to know that the murderer might be hanged; all that mattered was that he and the girl he loved were in an air-tight room, and that in a few hours that air would be exhausted.

He took off his shoe and hurled it with all his force at the glass above his head. For ten minutes he went on throwing it; then with a little gesture of despair he threw the shoe on the floor. The glass was too thick; he was only exhausting himself and using up precious oxygen uselessly.

"Supposing we shouted, Jack?" said the girl, quietly.

For a quarter of an hour they shouted "Help!" at intervals of half a minute. No one came; nothing happened.

"It's getting terribly stuffy, Jack," she whispered.

"Yes, darling; I'm afraid it is," he answered, steadily.

He was sitting on the arm of her chair—thinking desperately. Was there no way out? Was there nothing to be done?

"He can't mean to kill us like this," she cried, in despair.

He bent and kissed her gently, and she clung to him like a frightened child.

And so they sat for twenty minutes or more, till suddenly the girl clutched his arm.

"Jack," she whispered, "look up. Oh, my God, look at him!"

She cowered back in the chair, and the man beside her, strong-nerved though he was, shuddered uncontrollably. For staring down on them from above, with his face pressed against the glass, was Hubert Garling. He was crawling over the smooth surface like some loathsome insect—gloating as he watched them.

Moved by an uncontrollable impulse, Jack Denver seized his discarded shoe and hurled it at the madman. So straight was the aim that they could see him start back; then, as the shoe dropped harmlessly back to the floor, Garling's face once more pressed against the glass. And he was shaking with maniacal laughter.

"Turn off the light, dear," sobbed the girl. "I can't bear it."

There was a click and the tower was in darkness.

"Hold me in your arms, darling," she cried, pitifully. "I'm not frightened when you've got me close."

Jack Denver took her in his arms almost mechanically: into his mind had come an idea. Above them, outlined against the sky, they could see Garling, and it seemed as if he was beating furiously against the glass with his fists, enraged at being baulked of his triumph.

"Listen, sweetheart," said Jack, urgently. "There's a chance. Just a chance. If he thinks we're dead it's possible he might come in and open the door. I want you to sprawl forward on the floor—face downwards. Don't move. Just lie there. Then I'll switch on the light, stagger round the room once or twice, and then fall myself. Act, my beloved, act as you have never acted before."

"I understand, dear," she answered, steadily. "Just kiss me once more." He strained her to him; then she lay down on the floor half hidden by the desk.

"Ready, Hilda?"

"Yes, Jack; I'm ready."

Once more the light went on, and Jack Denver stared upwards. Act—oh, God!—let him act sufficiently to deceive the madman. He plucked at his collar, and staggered wildly back against the desk; then he raised imploring hands to Garling. His breath came in short gasps; he went to the door and beat on it. Then again he raised his hands towards the gibbering, gloating face, transformed now with a sort of a diabolical ecstasy into something utterly fiendish.

Then he pitched forward on his face—turned over, and lay staring through half-closed eyes at the man above. Had they bluffed him? Garling's face was still pressed against the glass; his eyes roamed from one to the other of his victims.

A quarter of an hour—eternity—went by, and he was still there. And then quite suddenly he was gone; the stars shone through the dome clear and unimpeded. For five minutes Jack Denver remained motionless; then, still lying in the same position, he spoke in a whisper.

"He's gone, darling; but don't move yet. If he comes in, I'll go for him, but whatever happens you get on the other side of the door."

"All right, Jack; but pray Heaven he comes soon. I don't think I can go on much longer."

Again eternity passed: the door was still shut. He wasn't coming; the acting had been in vain. Hubert Garling had seen, as he thought, their agony before they became unconscious; now he was going to make quite certain they were dead before he bothered with them further.

And with a dreadful feeling of physical sickness Jack Denver realized that, though the acting had been in vain, it had been a wonderful dress-rehearsal. Even so, in reality, would Hilda pitch forward and lie still; even so would he tear at his collar and fight for the air which was not there.

The girl had risen, and he rose too, and went to her.

"He's not coming, Jack," she said, steadily. "We've failed."

"Yes, dear—I'm afraid we've failed."

"So this is the end."

He made no answer; only put his arm round her waist and held her tightly.

"I'm not frightened, my man," she went on, quietly. "I expect I'll go first, but you'll find me waiting for you over the other side of the valley."

He cried aloud in his agony of mind; already he felt as if an iron band was pressing round his head.

"Oh, God!—if I could only get a message through somehow."

And even as his prayer went up, his eyes rested on the electric light switch. He'd seen it fifty times before; he'd used it in that last despairing throw for safety; and now—he stared at it as if he'd seen it for the first time. Fool that he was—idiot, not to have thought of it before. The tower could be seen from the road, even if he couldn't be heard from there. And it was the only chance. He turned off the light; then he began to signal.

Three short bursts of light; three long ones; three short again. S.O.S. Then HELP in Morse. Again and again S.O.S. HELP. S.O.S. HELP.

And the iron band round his head grew tighter and tighter. How long he went on he had no idea; time was measured only by the click of the switch—on and off. Dimly he realized that the girl had got to her feet, and with a dreadful look in her face was staggering towards him. He felt her clutch hold of his arm; from a great distance he heard her voice:

"Jack—I can't breathe; I can't———"

Her grip relaxed, and she collapsed on the floor at his feet, struggling horribly to breathe.

S.O.S. HELP. S.O.S. HELP.

Slower and slower the message flashed out into the night, until, at last, it ceased altogether. And Jack Denver's knees gave from under him. With one last effort he turned off the light; then he crumpled up on the floor beside the woman he loved.

And so they found them—two naval officers, one of whom, by the mercy of Allah, was a doctor.

"My God!" he gasped, as they flung open the door and the atmosphere inside hit them. "Get 'em into the fresh air, Flags; and for Heaven's sake—hurry."

"Are they dead, Doc?" cried his companion, as they laid the two unconscious bodies by an open window.

"No—but damned near it." He looked thoughtfully at his brother officer. "Go down and see what's happened to that madman below, old boy. I'll look after these two."

The Flag-Lieutenant went, to return in a few moments with a face that was strangely white.

"Doc.," he muttered, "he's dead. Halfway along the passage there."

The doctor got up quickly and followed the other. And for a while he stood looking at Hubert Garling's face, that stared with unseeing eyes at the ceiling.

"Heart, Flags, or I'm a Dutchman," he said. "The struggle to get the key did for him."

They covered the distorted face with a pocket-handkerchief, and went back to the living. And it was a couple of minutes before either of them spoke again.

"May Heaven be praised, old man," said the doctor, "that we decided to motor back to Portsmouth and not stop in town. It strikes me there have been some funny things happening here tonight."

"Where the devil are the servants, anyway?" demanded his pal.

"We'll get them shortly," said the other. "And the police, too. Don't forget, old man, we killed that bloke between us. It was the only thing to do: he was crazy. But it's a police matter."

"What is?" Jack Denver's hoarse croak made them both swing round. He was sitting up, swaying a little, and the doctor hurried to him.

"Feeling better?" he said. "That's good."

Denver pushed him away.

"How's Hilda—how's Mrs. Garling?"

"Going fine. She hasn't come round yet—but she will soon. There she is, beside you."

For a moment Denver looked at her, then he got up unsteadily.

"I don't know who you are," he said, "but there's a man in this house I'm going to kill."

The two naval officers looked at one another.

"Steady, old chap," said the Flag-Lieutenant. He followed Denver along the passage. "Unless I'm much mistaken, he's dead already."

They paused by the body, and he lifted the pocket-handkerchief from the dead man's face.

"Is that the man?"

"It is," said Denver. "How did it happen?"

"It doesn't take long to tell," answered the other. "We were motoring back from town, and suddenly we saw your signals. At first we paid no attention, and then—being a Flag-Lieutenant myself—I took them in automatically. S.O.S. Help. We rushed into the house and found that man in the hall downstairs. He was crazy—or so it seemed to us. Told us you were dead by now: and if you weren't you were going to die. Brandished a key in front of our faces, and roared with laughter. We were on him like a knife, and, I can tell you, he put up a fight. But we got the key, and we got to you in time."

"She's coming to," said the doctor's voice from just behind them.

For a moment Jack Denver stared at them both.

"I won't try and thank you now," he said, quietly. "I'll do that and explain everything shortly. But when you've been into the valley of the shadow with someone, and come out first, it's good to welcome your fellow-voyager."

He turned and went back to Hilda Garling. And when, a few seconds later, she opened her eyes, it was into his that they stared. His arms were round her, and he was smiling.

"Jack," she whispered, exultingly, "it wasn't so terrible, was it? And we're together after all."

For a moment he didn't understand: then it came to him.

"Dear heart," he said, tenderly. "We're not dead: we're alive."

Milton Keynes UK
Ingram Content Group UK Ltd.
UKHW030744071024
449371UK00006B/564